KNOWLEDGE AND INITIATION

COGNITION OF THE CHRIST THROUGH ANTHROPOSOPHY

Two lectures by
RUDOLF STEINER
London, April 14 and 15, 1922

STEINER BOOK CENTRE
151 Carisbrooke Crescent
North Vancouver, V7N 2S2
Canada

ISBN 0-919924-21-2

Rudolf Steiner's lectures to English audiences, spoken in German, were usually divided into three parts and immediately translated into English by George Adams, whose capacity for a precise interpretation was truly remarkable.
The following two lectures are shorthand records of these simultaneous translations and edited by comparing them with the texts of the original German.
The lectures were given to an audience familiar with Anthroposophy. The reader, who has no prior acquaintance with Anthroposophy, can gain the necessary background by reading Rudolf Steiner's books: "Knowledge of the Higher Worlds and its attainment" and "Theosophy".

The original German texts of these lectures are published under the title: Das Sonnenmysterium und das Mysterium von Tod und Auferstehung (Vol. 211 in the Bibliographical Survey, 1961.).

All rights reserved

Printed in Canada

ISBN 0-919924-21-2

KNOWLEDGE AND INITIATION

Anthroposophy, as I am attempting to expound it, represents a science of initiation originating in the necessity of the day. A science of initiation has existed always. Anthroposophy springs from the same foundation as ancient science, but in the course of human evolution ages succeed each other and vary in their demands. And thus the science of initiation arising out of the modern spirit is in some respects peculiar to this age, just as there was an initiation science of the Middle Ages, of Ancient Greece and of yet older periods of human evolution.

In the course of history the whole constitution and mood and tendency of the human soul undergoes changes. The so-called science of initiation has to investigate and understand what is the eternal in the human being and in the universe. We have to consider the needs and the sub-conscious longings of today, and a science of initiation, an ancient science that meets those needs and longings, is what Anthroposophy strives for.

It is for that very reason that it meets with such opposition, for the present time, standing as it does in the midst of the thoughts of natural science, is filled with certain judgments and prejudices which very often prevent us from consciously recognizing the sub-conscious longings within. And yet, if we regard life without bias, we have to understand that the conceptions of external natural science do not reach to what is eternal in the human being and in the universe. When, on the other hand, we of to-day turn aside from the external thoughts of natural science and attempt to find the eternal by inner mystic contemplation, we may indeed reach to a certain amount of faith or belief, but we do not attain that clear knowledge which to-day is necessary. Between these two extremes Anthroposophy has to take its stand. So it is that Anthroposophy is so generally misunderstood, because it endeavours in accordance with modern needs to attain to a science of initiation which is exact and of the nature of knowledge, and not of the nature of vague kinds of mysticism. But to understand what are the unconscious longings and needs of our time is to understand the need for such a thing as Anthroposophy.

I am not dwelling any longer on this introductory aspect because I assume that those who are here this evening have already experienced two things: that our natural scientific thoughts — borrowed from natural science and modelled upon it — do not reach far enough to penetrate and place before us the eternal in man and in the world, and that mysticism only reaches in a vague and unclear way and therefore, in that sense, is insufficient to meet present needs. One could prove these things by a multitude of examples if one were to dwell upon them further. Anthroposophy seeks for what may be called exact clairvoyance, again to borrow a term from scientific usage; that is to say it seeks to develop a knowledge and perception of the spiritual worlds which is no less exact, no less conscientious in the sense of exact science, than is the best tendency and striving of our natural scientific age.

I shall now indicate briefly how this path is begun. We must consider in the first place what we know in the ordinary life of the soul by means of our ordinary self-knowledge as the three forces or faculties that work in the soul, viz., thinking, feeling, and willing. We know in our thoughts that we are, as it were, awake; that we are essentially wakeful human beings. It is by virtue of our thinking life, which ceases between going to sleep at night and regaining consciousness in the morning, that we are awake, and it is in our thoughts that our soul-life is filled with a kind of clarity, an inner light.

Next as to the feeling life. The feelings are perhaps even more important for the human being (or he attaches more importance to them) than are his thoughts, but we know from our ordinary observation that the feelings of our soul-life are far less clear and filled with light than our thoughts. In a sense our thoughts, our conceptual life, play into our feelings and bring them into a certain clarity, but our feelings seem to surge up from the unknown depths of our life. They do not appear with the full clearness of our life of thought.

Then we come to the third category of our soul-life, the impulses of will. Our impulses of will come from still deeper down and are still less clear and have less light. But from what we know already in the observation of our ordinary life about thinking, feeling and willing, we realize at once how little we know of what is happening within us; for example, when an impulse of will arises making us take some action! We realize how little we know of what is happening in that life of will itself, and yet we find that thinking, feeling and willing still form a kind of unity in our soul-life. At the one pole is our conceptual life, our thinking life, we find in the way in which we join the concepts together like the links of a chain that there is an element of will at work in the process. Then passing to the other pole, the life of will — for the feeling life stands midway between the two — we find that for willing there is a certain element of conception; the concepts play into our willing life. So we see that in our soul-life there are the two poles, thinking on the one hand and willing on the other, with feeling as it were between the two, and that in these three something works in them all.

Now with the development of a higher science, the science of initiation, according to modern requirements and to Anthroposophy, it is necessary to train, develop and evolve by our own conscious activity both the conceptual thinking-life and the will-life, and it is thus that we can trace what has been called an exact clairvoyance, a modern science of initiation. In the one case we have to carry out exercises in thought, and in the other of will. So it is that the way is sought to pass through those portals which lead into the super-sensible worlds; indeed without entering those worlds in consciousness it is impossible to gain that clear knowledge we need of the eternal in the soul and in the universe.

It is while taking the exercises in thought that special attention has to be paid to what is not generally observed in ordinary life, viz., that slight additional element of will which is playing into the thinking life. This subject is dealt with in much greater detail in my book that is translated into English under the title *Knowledge of the Higher Worlds and How to Attain It*. We have above all to train that element of will which is at work in our thinking life, and in a sense have to exercise it. We have to select that very thing which passes unnoticed in the ordinary everyday thought-life, and pay less attention to what is most important to us in that life. We have to form a clear concept in our minds — its content is not of much importance; it may be either a simple or a complex concept — and then hold it as the full content of the soul to the exclusion of all else. To do this calls forth the full energy of the soul and an exercise of strong will power. The selected concept must be clearly abstracted for a certain time from everything else in the world, so that the forces of the soul are concentrated upon it alone. In the case of one individual these exercises may have to be carried on for months, in the case of another years, but sooner or later, provided they are undertaken systematically and with persistent energy, the soul-life will develop and experience an inner strengthening. What happens may be compared with the effect produced by exercising a certain muscle, by its doing the work for which it is best fitted, until it is developed to its full power. After a time has elapsed (varying, as we have seen, according to the individual) there will come a certain moment when the soul will have an experience of such strength and power that it will be shaken to its very foundations.

This experience may be described somewhat as follows: with the strengthening of the soul-life the door is opened to an entirely new way of thinking and to entirely new thoughts. It may be compared with the way in which sense impressions and thoughts are experienced in the ordinary soul-life. How do we experience sense impressions? In all sense impressions such as those of colour and sound, heat and cold, there is a certain vitality and life; they are experienced in a very living way and in the full sap of life. But in the way in which the thoughts are experienced there is something abstract, something vague and sketchy in outline; it is all grey and pale as compared with the intensity and living nature of the sense experiences. Now, when this new way of thinking has been attained, we find that the whole thought-life has become as intense and as full of life as is the ordinary soul-life in sense experiences and perceptions. It is called imaginative thinking; imaginative not in the sense of arbitrary fantasies in the mind but a pictorial, formative thought filled with inner life and possessing a quality of strength and intensity comparable with the sense impressions of the ordinary life. And with this life of imaginative thought, which is saturated with a kind of plastic vitality, there comes the realization that within us is an entirely new human being of which we never knew consciously before. The ordinary physical human being may be described as an 'organism in space'; we see the different organs spread out in space, so to speak, and know that they are all connected together, that the heart is connected with the whole and the right hand with the left and so forth. The new human being that we come to know within us in the life of imaginative thought, however, is better described as 'an organism in time'. Suddenly there stands before us in a single imaginative tableau or picture a memory of our whole life; in the first place to a point in early childhood; not, however, in the way in which isolated memories of the past appear more or less dully in the ordinary consciousness, but as the whole individual life laid out before us in a single moment. In this sense we, as human beings, are time-organisms. We have come to experience what in the modern science of initiation are called the 'formative forces of the body'; not the full human being, using the term body in its extended sense, but its formative forces which in the older science of initiation are called the ether or etheric body. So we come to experience something that works within and builds up the physical organism of man; to know that when we entered this life in the physical body of a child we brought with us certain super-sensible forces direct from the super-sensible world; to know that these forces were modelling and moulding our physical organs, our minds, the circulation of our blood, even in our earliest childhood, and were gradually taking possession of the whole of our organism stage by stage. In the space-organism of the physical body the formative forces of the etheric body were building all the time. With this experience comes also an understanding of how we enter this world with certain particular faculties and qualities of character, and of how one individual will develop in quite a different direction from another. This knowledge of what works in our physical organism as a super-sensible thing brings us to the stage of the exact higher knowledge which the present age needs as its science of initiation. Thus to know the formative forces or etheric body from imaginative knowledge is the first and necessary stage we must pass through before we can learn to know what is essentially the eternal which was working in the human being in the spiritual worlds before birth.

As we have to learn to carry the power of will into our thoughts, and to strengthen that power in the holding of thoughts with the full forces of the soul, so we then have to carry out exercises in the opposite direction. We have to attain the power to extract the soul from the concept that we have learned to hold to the exclusion of everything else, so that they fill our consciousness, and then to extract ourselves from them so that our consciousness is empty of content and yet we maintain our wakefulness.

Now let us consider our ordinary life. Here our consciousness is always filled with thoughts, sense perceptions and memories, and the moment they cease to be there we tend to drop into sleep. Therefore it needs a still greater activity, a greater power, to hold the soul in full wakefulness when it is rendered empty of what has been held within it by imagination and concentration. This power is attained in the next stage if, by means of the exercises referred to earlier, we have once attained the power to hold a concept in our consciousness to the exclusion of all else. It consists in being able to detach the soul from the particular concept leaving the consciousness empty of content and yet wakeful, and once this is acquired there enters into the emptied but wakeful consciousness something which is entirely new to us, something which is not of the nature of a reflection, a memory or a conception, but a super-sensible reality. It floods into the soul, this spiritual reality of being which is in all the individual things of the world, and we see it blossoming forth from everything in nature. Into the consciousness that we have had the strength to train through meditation and concentration, and then to empty of content while keeping it fully wakeful, there streams the reality of spiritual being so that we perceive the super-sensible reality of being in the world. This is the super-sensible reality of which Anthroposophy and the science of initiation speak, not as of a vague 'beyond' but of something that is present, that is certainly outside the world of the senses and not perceived therein. So we may learn to penetrate into an entirely new thinking, to see that whereas our ordinary thought is making use of the time and the instruments of the physical brain and the nervous system, this new thinking is independent of the physical organism and outside it. It is this higher knowledge that is attained by the science of initiation from the conditions of the ordinary knowledge which is connected with the physical instruments of the physical brain and nervous system.

There is yet another faculty of soul in which the student of the higher knowledge must train himself. It is that faculty which we know in ordinary life as presence of mind, the power to meet a circumstance that comes upon us suddenly and, without spending a long time in deliberation, to perceive the right course immediately. This faculty must be developed and enhanced, so that he who has these experiences before him in the super-sensible world, shall be able to grasp the reality of the spiritual world as it flits past. He must have the presense of mind to recognize it at once.

Now by the exercising and training of the soul to attain the power of detaching it from the content of consciousness, and of holding it empty and yet fully awake, we are led to perceive something still higher than was explained in the first part of this lecture. We are led to what is essentially the soul and spiritual being of man that had lived in the spiritual worlds before it united with the physical substance of heredity, with the physical bodily substance, for the course of this earthly life. We come to know our own eternal being, our life of soul and spirit in the spiritual worlds before birth. This second stage of knowledge is known as inspired or inspirational knowledge, as a technical term in this modern science of initiation. Just as the outer air enters our lungs through inhalation so does the spiritual world enter into our emptied consciousness. Thus we inhale, so to speak, the spiritual world as we knew it before we descended into physical earth existence. So we learned to know one facet of our being, the other side is the spiritual immortality. This will be dealt with in the third part of this lecture. We come to know in this second stage, but to know clearly, what might be defined as the 'birthlessness' or 'unbornness' (just as we speak of deathlessness or immortality) of that other side of the eternal in man, viz., that which existed in the spiritual worlds, his life in those worlds before birth. Our present age has very few conceptions, even though it may have dim conceptions through faith, about immortality, but in this second stage we learn to know our birthlessness, our eternal on the other side, our life in the spiritual reality before we entered this particular earthly life.

This higher 'inspired knowledge' leads us also in another direction which however can only be touched upon here, since it would take many lectures to describe it in detail. Just as we learn to know the super-sensible, the eternal reality of our own being, and to enter through inspired knowledge into our own soul and spirit before we entered this physical life, so do we learn to recognize the spirit in the world around us. This must be described in a few short sketches. If we look out upon the universe the sun appears to us as a physical ball, but when we enter into 'inspirational knowledge' we see it not only as the concentrated physical object that is seen by the senses. We see something that spreads through the whole universe and is accessible to us, namely, the spiritual quality and being of the sun, the sun-like being itself. What we see everywhere in mineral, in plant and animal, what is in man too as sun-force that we see physically concentrated when we look up to the sun. Though it may sound strange from the point of view of modern science, what we thus attain through inspirational knowledge is the power to perceive this sun-like being in everything, in the mineral, the plant, the animal and the human being. We learn to perceive the sun-force working in every single organ, in the heart, the liver and so forth, of the physical organism, and in everything within the whole universe that is accessible to us. This is the actual reality that is attained through the science of initiation.

And out of inspiration-knowledge we see that just as the sun does not only have a sharp outline, the same applies to the moon. The external physical moon is only the physical concentration, while the moon-substance streams through the whole universe. It is in mineral, plant and animal and every organ of man, in them the moon- and sun-substances live on. This experience comes in the second stage of inspirational knowledge, and it leads to something which is eminently practical and which already has been developed as a science, viz., the anthroposophical science of medicine. By its means we learn to see how in every human organ there is a kind of balance between the sun-force and the moon-force, the sun-substance and the moon-substance. In the former we recognize that there is something that expresses itself in the life element, in the blossom and growth of youthful forces, and in the moon-force something that expresses itself in degeneration and ageing, in the thinning down of those blossoming, living forces which we can describe as a spiritual reality, as the sun-force. We recognize that there is a kind of balance and that both forces, both qualities of being which are at work permeating every single organ, are necessary; we see how that when we are sick it is because there is a preponderance, an inbalance of the one force over the other. Hence it becomes possible to exercise a healing influence on this or that organ of a sick human being by bringing to bear upon it the particular forces that are at work in some plant or mineral from the external world; the preponderance of one force at work in the sick man is counteracted by a particular plant or mineral in which the opposite spiritual force is at work. So we attain to a definite and rational science of medicine, and one that has not merely collected a number of empirical results but is built up scientifically upon rational conceptions.

I have shown how we can come to a true self-knowledge, how this can also help us in practical life. I have shown this for one field of activity, it is also possible to do the same for others. So we can say: initiation science provides on the one hand the basis for the deepest longings of the human soul; on the other, gives us what we need to work practically in the world, but deeper than through external science. This second aspect of human knowledge leads to the Spirit of the Cosmos. Higher still is that which leads us to conscious knowledge of man's passing through the gate of death.

It is only when this inspirational knowledge is attained that we come to perceive and recognize in full consciousness, the inner soul nature of our own human being. We then recognize our reality, the reality of our existence purely in soul, that is to say, independently of the body, for we recognize how we lived without a physical body in the spiritual worlds before birth.

Having thus dealt with the inspirational knowledge that brings us experience of our spiritual life before birth, I now come to the third stage of higher knowledge, that which leads us to conscious knowledge of the passing through the gate of death to immortality.

This knowledge of the soul-spiritual of man remains one-sided if there is progress only up to inspired knowledge, before birth. To obtain knowledge of life after death, the exercises to develop supersensible knowledge must be raised to a still higher degree. This time, just as to start with, the element of will was trained and carried into the life of thought which thus became strengthened, so now it is a matter of carrying the thoughts into the life of will. For example, suppose that in the evening we set ourselves to think over the events and experiences of the day that is past, not however by beginning with the morning and following out the events in the order in which they took place, but beginning with those that were the most recent and tracing them backwards. What is the effect of this exercise of following the events of the day in the opposite way from their natural sequence? In our ordinary life and experience our thoughts all the while are being moulded and conditioned and determined by the course of our experiences in 'time'; as they occur so do our thoughts take their impression. Whereas in those exercises whereby we pass from one event or experience to another in the reverse order we are training a strong element of will, not in the way that is determined by the external events or experiences but in the opposite way. By this means we develop strong forces of will and carry the thinking life into the willing life. It may be done by remembering a tune or melody backwards, or by following the action of a drama from the fifth Act back to the first. It may at first only be possible to pick out isolated episodes during the day, but gradually the power is attained of having the whole of the day's experiences before us in a kind of picture, passing backwards from the evening to the morning. Thus do we drive the power of thought right down into our will-life.

Further, the will-life should be trained so strongly that not only do we go about our life with those qualities and faculties and characteristics which we already had in childhood, or gained through education; we also carry on a rigorous self-education as mature men and women, especially if we set ourselves deliberately to train one or other specific quality or characteristic wherein we are lacking, and to develop along those lines, no matter if the exercises take a number of years. Thus by self-education we train ourselves to will, until we come to pass into the supersensible world from yet another side. This may be explained as follows. Think of our soul life; what is our volitional life like? For instance, we have a certain conception, and as a result we wish, let us say, to raise our arm; a conception and then an act of will. But we have no knowledge of the way in which we raise our arm; that will-process by means of which we pass from conception to action is entirely hidden from us. We are asleep, so to speak, in our will life, and we are awake in our conceptual and inner thought-life. By way of comparison, how is it that the eye enables us to see the external world? It becomes transparent, and by thus practising a sort of self abnegation enables us to see right through it to the world. So much for the physical sense, but in a sense of soul the whole of our organism must be made transparent so that we learn to look on our physical organism in a physical sense and in a sense more transparent.

Then do we come to experience the moment of death. When we have attained the power, through these exercises of the soul, of making our physical body transparent, we have before us a picture of the moment of death and we pass in conscious experience out through the gate of death and experience our immortality. This is the stage of Intuitive knowledge, the true intuitive knowledge. We know that once we have reached this stage after passing through Imagination and Inspiration, that we then belong to the universe as an eternal being, that we behold the spirit in the universe with the eternal spirit in us. That is the plateau initiation science reaches when it adapts to modern consciousness. In old times it rose in us in an atavistic, dreamlike way, but today it has to be in full consciousness, from the transitory to the eternal.

The conclusion should not be drawn that this science of initiation is only of importance to those who immediately set out to acquire these higher faculties of knowledge which have been described as imagination, inspiration and intuition. No. It is necessary for every human being, but just as it is not given to every man to become a painter so it is with this science. Everyone with a healthy and unbiased artistic sense can understand and appreciate a painting, and in the same way those who through the science of initiation have attained imaginational, inspirational and intuitional knowledge of the spiritual world, can describe that knowledge to their fellow men. And when once shown it can be understood by those who will exercise the simple unbiased faculties of thought and judgment normal to our present stage of development; such people can then take their stand upright as human beings equal to the tasks of life in the present age.

We must not meet this science of initiation with all sorts of prejudices and all sorts of confusions arising out of the prejudices and habits of thought and judgment that are external. For example, we must not confuse it with any kind of vision and hallucination, for it is outside and beyond the visionary, hallucinatory, or the mystical experiences. Imagination, inspiration and intuition are the very opposite of such. What is the characteristic of hallucinatory and visionary experience? It is that the person is completely given up to his visions and hallucinations; dependent upon them and therefore unable to maintain his full independence. But when undergoing this higher training of the soul that has been described, when we are developing this higher knowledge, imagination, inspiration and intuition in the soul, all the time there is standing beside us, fully present and fully there, the ordinary human being with his feet on the ground, his firm and sound judgment unhampered, entirely capable of exercising criticism, and with the full presence of mind of the ordinary healthy human being at the present stage. We are not completely given up and lost in these spiritual experiences but maintain full control; standing beside us is a normal and healthy human being.

Anthroposophy is actually a continuation of that modern striving for knowledge which has led to the results of natural science with its achievements of external scientific knowledge. This the anthroposophist would by no means decry, but would maintain that the results of external science need to be supplemented and completed, in the present experience and stage of the world, by a science extending into the higher spiritual worlds. In that sense it is a continuation of the true striving for knowledge of our age, and despite the triumphs of natural science it may well be said by those with a heart and an understanding of the experiences of the modern world, that the need of men for this higher knowledge is being proclaimed on every side. One may speak, for instance, of the need for higher knowledge in the religious and moral and ethical demands of the human soul. The subject that will be dealt with in the following lecture is the application of this science of initiation to an understanding of the Mystery of Golgotha.

In conclusion, just as we see the external features and physiognomy of a man confronting us but do not know him well until we become his friend, entering into his life with heart and soul until we know him from within, so it is with the natural science that we have attained so far. For it shows the external features or physiognomy of the world, and the need of the world and of humanity to-day is to gain a knowledge that not only shows those things but enters into the spiritual and soul-life of the universe. It is that which this higher knowledge of initiation reaches; something that perceives the spiritual and soul-being in all the universe and in the human being himself. In that sense and to develop to its real completion, the fundamental striving for knowledge, this science of initiation springing from the needs and from the spirit of the age in which we live and whose tasks we have to accomplish.

friends and members in many countries the movement has been able to build the Goetheanum, its headquarters at Dornach, near Basle, Switzerland,* as an independent school of anthroposophical science. And in all its forms this building expresses that same deep spiritual reality which finds utterance through the spoken and the written word for the ideas and thoughts of the science.

Had any other spiritual movement in our time required to build a headquarter it would have commissioned an architect to design it on Antique, Renaissance or Gothic lines, or in one of the prevailing styles. This the anthroposophical Movement, by reason of its inner nature, could not do. The architectural forms of the Goetheanum are drawn from the same source out of which the ideas of the supersensible spring, as they are proclaimed through the world. Everything that is found in Dornach, be it sculpture or painting, is carried by a new style out of which Anthroposophy is born in this modern age. Whoever visits this School for Spiritual Science will find that on the one hand the anthroposophical world view is proclaimed from the rostrum in words and on the other hand the forms of the building and the paintings express in an artistic way what is expressed by the word. That which can work from the stage should only be another form of revelation than that what can be effected through the word. Anthroposophy should come out of the deepest foundations of humanity, of which theoretical Anthroposophy is only one branch, education and the arts are the others. In this way anthroposophical life becomes a factor in the most varied fields of human existence. The Waldorf School, which has been founded in Stuttgart, is not in any sense a school where children are taught a particular anthroposophical conception of the world. It is one where the teachers themselves, not so much in what they teach as in how they do so and in the whole way in which they exercise the art of education — are permeated in their faculties with that which anthroposophy can give them. Reference could be made to other directions in which the

*Refers to the first Goeteanum, destroyed by fire on December 31, 1922. Rebuilt as the present Goetheanum. (Ed.)

modern science of initiation is proving itself of use in every branch of human life and activity. Moreover it operates upon and vitalizes the religious needs of civilized humanity, and as these needs are deeply connected with an understanding of the Mystery of Golgotha it is with that subject that I propose to deal now.

Let me begin by connecting what I have to say with what was said yesterday about the path of spiritual development for modern times leading to imagination, inspiration and intuition. I showed how by imagination and concentration, by means of certain exercises, the student can develop his thought-power until it becomes something which may be called imaginative in the real sense of the word, and in such a way that thought becomes not what it ordinarily is — abstract, cold, and in outline sketchy if compared with the intense vitality of sense impressions — but imaginative, pictorial, vivid and full of life, and in these characteristics no way inferior to impressions of the senses. The man who has attained to imaginative thinking, has something as full of life as when in normal daily existence he yields to the impressions of the world of colour or of sound.

But between the students of the new science of initiation who attain to this imaginative thought, and those who abandon themselves to uncontrolled vision and hallucination, there is an important difference. The man who is subject to visions and hallucinations is not aware that the pictures which arise before him are subjective; on the other hand, he who has imaginative thought is fully aware that what he has before him is not an external reality but is something subjective having its origin in his own inner life. He knows the subjective nature of that imaginative picture-world. He knows too, that when through 'imaginative thought' he comes to perceive what was called yesterday his 'time organism' — the formative force body that works within the physical body as its sculptor and architect — he is perceiving the first spiritual super-sensible thing that he can experience, and something that essentially belongs to his own inner being.

Then there comes the second stage on that path of development when he becomes so strong that he is not only able to concentrate the full forces of his soul at will upon the concepts, and then upon the imaginative pictures he has before him in imaginative thought, but can divert that picture world away from his consciousness while maintaining it in a fully wakeful condition. He is now ready for the real imaginations to pour into him from the external world spiritually, speaking through the outside spiritual universe, i.e., the objective imaginations as against the subjective picture-world that he had before. Here is attained the stage I have described as inspirational knowledge. He perceives his own spiritual being as it exists independently of his physical bodily organism, and as it existed in the worlds of soul and spirit before he entered into this physical life through conception and birth. He has before him a picture of his prenatal existence in the spiritual world and of the spiritual realities of the whole universe, and comes in contact through conscious knowledge with the spiritual reality of man and of the universe. Thus, through this imaginative, inspirational knowledge, he discovers what he was before he descended into this physical incarnation in a physical body for this life. He discovers also that when he came down from the spiritual worlds he carried with him into this physical life the power of thought which he here possesses in his ordinary consciousness. What is this power of thought? It is that which he already had in his life in the spiritual worlds before birth, but ordinary consciousness only shows it in a pale and abstract outline.

He then comes to recognize something that may be thus described: he gazes upon the picture at the gate of death, and the moment of death, and sees that the physical body is no longer held together and built up in its whole forces by the force of an indwelling human soul but is given over to the forces of the earth as they work in the external mineral world; he sees how, through decay or the process of burning, the human physical body is given up to those mineral forces and assimilated with the earth. He sees by comparison how, in effect, what is carried into the earthly life through birth is something (speaking now in the sense of the soul) that dies into the physical body just as the latter dies into the earth at death. What he had in his power of thought in the ordinary consciousness was something that was vital and full of spiritual life in the spiritual worlds before conception and birth, but was then killed in the physical body so that it appeared in ordinary consciousness as the power of deadened thought.

Because of this fact knowledge of today is so unsatisfactory for man, as he comprehends, in a certain sense, only lifeless nature. It is an illusion when he thinks that through scientific experiments he can reach anything else. Certainly there will be progress beyond representing only lifeless nature; they will be able to create organic substances. But it will not be understood by the deadened thinking, even when they have been created in the laboratories. With this kind of thinking, which is the corpse of the soul which is spiritually dead, only death can be understood.

In what then does the process consist that was described as the development of the soul to imaginative, inspirational and intuitional knowledge? It is in effect this, that we call to life within ourselves what was killed in our power of thought. When we develop the living, imaginative, plastic thought, and inspirational and intuitional cognition, we call to life our power of thought, which was dead.

We have now reached the point where we should be able to understand human evolution and history. Modern scientific history usually skims over the surface of external events, without regarding the metamorphoses that go on within the soul of man from age to age. We may ask why is it that in this age humanity has had to pass through a period when thought was abstract and of a deadened quality. The answer is that the full, living, spiritual thought, by its very vitality and fullness of life, exercises a kind of compulsion on the human soul. It is by passing through this dead and abstract thought that humanity has been able to achieve freedom, and for the evolution and development of freedom this stage was a necessary one.

After man has attained to Imagination and Inspiration, he has to say to himself: Something has happened to me, which causes me anxiety. I mention this as an unusual fact, for the strange thing happens, that the man of today when he has risen to Imagination and Inspiration, experiences real anxiety. This stems from the fact that today, when he becomes clairvoyant, man has to say to himself: I have become too strongly egotistical through my development. Anxiety arises in the heart and mind (Gemüt), for man has the feeling that his ego works too strongly. In ancient initiation, before the Mystery of Golgotha, the candidate went through the opposite experience: As he attained to initiation he found that in a sense he was becoming less ego-conscious, that he was pouring himself out into the universe and becoming less in possession of himself. His ego-consciousness was rather weakened than strengthened.

The turning point between these two characteristics of initiation is the Mystery of Golgotha. The first human being to pass through initiation, and to experience this deeply disquieting feeling when the ego becomes too strong, was St. Paul at Damascus. The passage in the New Testament (Acts 9) is so well known as to need no further reference here. It was on that occasion that he gained insight into the necessity for weakening the power of his ego; he realized that the initiate of the new age stood in need of a force to weaken the intensity of the ego-life, and as a result of his experience he pronounced the words which were to give the keynote to the whole development of humanity through initiation as from the moment of the Mystery of Golgotha. These words, which resounded forth into the future and pointed out the direction to be taken by the succeeding period of evolution, were 'Not I, but Christ in me.' When we look upon the place of Golgotha, and receive into ourselves the forces of the Christ Who descended to earth from the spiritual worlds and Who since the Mystery has permeated the earth, we are enabled to diminish the forces of the ego and to pass through initiation in the right way.

The abstract thinking of which I spoke in the first part of this lecture, where the power of thought is deadened and becomes like a soul-corpse living in the physical body, has prevailed only in the more recent times of human evolution. It began, gradually, some three or four centuries after the Mystery of Golgotha. In the more ancient people, man brought with him into his physical life out of the spiritual worlds more of the full life of thought which is now dead abstract thought. This may be confirmed by studying, without bias, the evolution of humanity and the records and experiences of man, whether initiate or non-initiate, in ancient times. Much is said today about so-called Animism, the poetic fancy of simple and primitive peoples, in an endeavour to explain the experiences of the past ages as recorded and handed down in tradition. But by facing up to realities we see that it was not in a kind of poetic fancy that ancient man described the woods and forests, lakes and mountains, springs, brooks, clouds and thunder and lightning, and everything physical in the world of Nature in a spiritual way. He saw and described not only the physical things that we see, but the spiritual beings that inhabited every flower and mineral, every spring and wood. That description was not, as in the modern conception of Animism, something created out of poetic fancy, but a direct experience of the living, spiritual power which man brought with him into physical life. It was as though, in a spiritual sense, he sent out feelers which felt and touched and realized, giving him experiences of the spiritual beings which inhabit everything in external nature. It is only since the third or fourth century after Christianity that gradually developed in humanity dead thinking, that dead consciousness which today can only see the mineral world. Ancient man experienced in himself something that was living; he was able to experience and to know the spiritual beings in the world and to recognize them as the same thing that had lived within him before he entered into the physical life. His experience was a very practical one, explaining his pre-natal existence in spiritual worlds, and he felt that something was born with him into this physical life and lived within him; he did not feel that this thought proceeded from the organism of his physical body, for he knew it was a living thing he had brought with him from the spiritual world before his birth.

Now we can quite well realize how the course of human evolution would have continued along the line that has been described, and how the thinking power of man would have become more and more dead. We can imagine evolution continuing in a straight downward line, and that is what would have happened if the Cross had not been raised upon Golgotha. Looking at the picture of death we see that had it not been for the Mystery of Golgotha the physical body of man would die, that his soul-life would die with his physical body. We can say out of our consciousness of this abstract, deadened thought, that our soul-life, i.e., our life of thought, partakes of death. And this is what humanity would have had to experience gradually more and more but for the Cross on Golgotha; no longer would there have been the living thought, but the soul-life would have slowly expired in universal death.

This is how we can regard the Mystery of Golgotha by means of the modern science of initiation, just as it is possible for those who are rooted in Christianity to regard the Mystery through the simple study of the Gospel records. This fresh aspect of the Mystery is the starting point for a new evolution and an upward one. He who goes through the experiences and training of the modern path of initiation, and who attains to inspirational and intuitive cognition, is able to attain to the point where a spiritual world is revealed, of which the Mystery of Golgotha is shown as the great solace in world existence. He also realizes that he has attained freedom, but as the price of that freedom he finds this deep and troubling experience, as he passes through the way of initiation to 'imagination' and 'inspiration', that his ego has been strengthened and intensified, and is now too strong. That is one pole of his experience. The other pole is that in spite of the strengthened ego he has gained from evolution he cannot save himself or mankind from the universal death of the soul-life. But when he looks out, from his spiritual experience in inspirational and intuitive cognition, upon the picture of the Cross on Golgotha, he sees that through the passing of that Divine Being, the CHRIST — first through the physical body of a human being, Jesus of Nazareth, and then through the gate of death — mankind can be redeemed from universal death. On the one hand man has strengthened the ego-consciousness, but this cannot save him from universal death; and on the other hand he sees redemption from that death in the picture of the Cross on Golgotha and of the dying and the risen Christ. Through this conscious spiritual knowledge he is able to understand from out of what experience the wonderful writers of the Gospels wrote. He sees that until the third or fourth century after Golgotha something still remained of that living thought in humanity, something of that spiritual world which man brought into his physical life, and that it was this which enabled isolated human beings in the first three or four centuries to understand the Mystery of Golgotha; even as the modern initiate can understand it by means of the new science of initiation when he goes through that path and through the exercises which have been described.

From the knowledge contained in the Gnosis — which resembles in some respects modern anthroposophical science — we find that in the first few centuries there was a certain understanding of the Mystery of Golgotha, and that unless that understanding had still existed in isolated human beings the Gospels never could have been written. They were written out of the last relics of the old prethinking purely through the forces of the soul.

This new thinking is so entirely different in its conditions from our ordinary life of thought that we may say we recognize for example that in this new spiritual perception, this spiritually perceptive thought, you have something in which there is no such thing as ordinarily you have in memory. In our ordinary life of thought, if it is healthy and sound at all, there is memory. If we learn a certain thought or concept we can call it to memory again. But in this super-sensible thinking, which does not make use of the physical organism, we cannot call back to mind; we have no memory of the experiences in this new thought we have had, and if we wish to return to it we must only remember the activity of soul, the exercises and the precise path which we took in inner activity and concentration of will in order to reach that particular knowledge or super-sensible concept. We can remember the path our soul took and we can repeat that path. Then that perception, that super-sensible knowledge, is freshly again before us. In the physical world if we have seen a rose, for example, and want to have it raised before us again in all its full colour and freshness, it is no use trying to remember it. No memory will restore what we received by our sense perception; we must come before the rose again. So in the higher super-sensible thinking to have our thoughts again before us in all their freshness we must return by the path that led us to them. Let me put this to you in a personal way. When I speak on the higher knowledge it is not from reading books on the subject or from hearing about it, but as one who has attained to and experienced it. If I give a lecture I cannot do so like one who speaks on external science, who simply has his knowledge systematized in his memory and then gives it out; I must pass through the full experiences, through all those qualities of feeling and of thought, of inner life and activity, through which I had to pass before I had gained that knowledge for the first time. I must speak from the full freshness of the past to give it full freshness in the present. So different are the conditions of

COGNITION OF THE CHRIST THROUGH ANTHROPOSOPHY

Clairvoyance, which is the basis of the modern science of initiation, has always existed. In the past ages it was something that rose up within the human being like an elemental force, and on the path of initiation those who had gone through fewer stages were essentially dependent for their progress upon the authority of those who had gone through more stages than they. But to meet the needs of the human soul of today we cannot build on authority; to do so would be to contradict the stage it has now reached.

In our age the methods are entirely built, as in external science, upon the continuous and full control of the individuality and personality; in the soul life there must be control in every stage and in every step taken by the new candidate for initiation. Hence in speaking of exact clairvoyance in connection with the modern science of initiation we use the word 'exact' as it is used in the term "exact" science. Yesterday I spoke of the insight we gain into the cosmos and into the working of all things through the modern science of initiation. That insight is by no means something which, when we study it, lives in the soul merely as a theory or an abstract conception; it is something which becomes a living, spiritual force which penetrates us fully in all our powers and faculties when we allow it to work upon us. Thus the anthroposophical spiritual movement has been made effective in many spheres of life and particularly in that of the artistic life. Through the help and self-sacrifice of its

Christian science of initiation. Hence we see why St. Paul out of his experience was able to say, 'Were it not for the risen Christ then all our faith and all our life of soul would have been in vain, would have remained dead'. Then we understand that the Divine Being, the God, descended to the earth and went through the gate of Death, and lives in and with the earth since the Mystery of Golgotha, and, as was not the case before, the forces of Christ are working especially in the evolution of humanity upon the earth. We know that He passed through and conquered death, that He rose again through conquering the death of the soul forces and redeemed the soul from death. And so are we able to enter our thinking life again, to enliven what has become dead in the soul-life by looking up from the deeply moving and troubling experience of our too much strengthened ego to the picture of the Mystery of Golgotha.

It is thus that anthroposophy can show the path, not away from Christ, but to Him. I shall now give an outline of what anthroposophical cognition tells us of the evolution of mankind in its approach to the Mystery of Golgotha.

In primeval times, when man's thinking was still alive and filled with spiritual vitality, he saw the spiritual alongside the physical being when he looked out upon the physical phenomena of the world of Nature. The spiritual thought he experienced in a somewhat dreamlike, instinctive consciousness, and he knew that his spiritual origin was in the spiritual worlds. From out of the great masses of men who thus knew instinctively of the spiritual world there arose individuals who gave themselves up to science, to the path of knowledge, just as in our time individuals become scientists and learned men. In that time when in the forces of all human souls there was still a connection with the spiritual world, there arose men of science and learning, initiates, who also by exercises and by training the soul (though different in character from those described for the modern science of development) attained to a kind of imagination, inspiration and intuition.

Intuition is the third stage of spiritual development. Here the initiate perceives not only pictures of the spiritual world, but enters into and communes with the spiritual beings themselves. In the spiritual worlds the initiates held a mighty and majestic communion with beings who descended from the divine spiritual worlds; they raised themselves to this inter-course. The most ancient and primeval teachers of humanity were spiritual beings who taught, not through the external senses and not by walking in physical bodies among men and teaching through the physical ear, but through the spiritual consciousness of the ancients. Now what was it primarily that these spiritual beings, the sublime teachers, taught mankind through these ancients? It was the mysteries of 'unbornness' of the human soul. They taught in clear knowledge that which was already known or felt instinctively by the masses of mankind, namely, how the life of man is connected in the spiritual worlds before birth. From these ancients, divine spiritual teachers, humanity learnt to know the destinies of the human soul through its connection with the life before birth. We can see how in ancient times death and resurrection were represented merely in pictorial form in the cults and ceremonies. The cults represented the death and the resurrection of gods, of divine beings, prophetically and in a picture that was not at that time a real and practical experience of the mysteries of death. For man had not then the same tragic experience of death as he has today; he still had within him the living life he had brought from the spiritual worlds into his physical life. Death to him did not mean that tragedy which it was to mean later when the soul-life had been drawn into the physical body and become like a corpse. In those ancient cults where death and resurrection of the Divine Being were represented as in a picture it was more like a pictorial prophecy of what was to come — the Mystery of Golgotha. The men who witnessed these cults and ceremonies were already able to say in dim prophecy that the god passes through death and conquers it, and that because the god conquers death so can the divine in the human soul. Nevertheless the pre-Christian mysteries and understandings and teachings of humanity by the divine spiritual beings was a teaching principally of the mysteries of birth not of death. And that is a deeply significant fact in the evolution of humanity.

The first initiates of the Christian era, looking upon the Mystery of Golgotha, recognized that the old initiation and the old teaching of the mysteries did not penetrate into the knowledge of death. They realized however that this knowledge was revealed in the Mystery of Golgotha. Then there was understood and was revealed what can only be described by saying literally that in the Mystery of Golgotha something happened which concerned the destinies of the gods themselves. It may be put in this way: looking down upon the earth, the divine spiritual beings could see that through a destiny that was beyond the power of the gods, the earth and humanity and all that was connected with humanity were being given up to death. But who was it that had no experience of death? The gods, the divine spiritual beings, those from whom the ancient primeval teachers of humanity descended to commune with the initiates when they had raised themselves to a consciousness of the spiritual. And they, the gods, did not partake in that death through which all earthly human beings were destined to pass. Therefore it was decided between the gods, not only as a matter concerning mankind but as one concerning the gods themselves, that a god should pass through the mystery of death on earth in a human body. That is the great mystery that we must understand about the Mystery of Golgotha. It not only concerns man but also the gods.

So it is that when we come to view the Mystery through the modern science of initiation our aspect or outlook is super-sensible. Anthroposophy leads to an understanding of this. Not only the initiate of today but every man may receive a stimulating impulse, encouragement and understanding from the modern science of initiation. We, all of us, may attain to an intensified and strengthened power of knowledge, and having done so may recognize that the Mystery of Golgotha which took place within earth-existence, was at the same time a cosmic and an earthly event. Then are we able to say, 'It is not I, but Christ in me Who makes me live again in the spiritual life of the soul.'

Anthroposophy does not lead to irreligion but to a religious life in the fullest sense of the term; we are deepened and penetrated with new spiritual forces. Through spiritual-scientific cognition of the Mystery of Golgotha man overcomes all doubts which are contained so strongly in today's religious life. External science has given us freedom, but with it has come doubt. It is the task of Anthroposophy to sweep away these doubts that have come in the train of external science and which were a necessary stage in the development of humanity, and because Anthroposophy is a spiritual science it is able to do so. It can instill into the heart and soul of man a religious sense for everything in the world and in mankind, and above all it can give an understanding of the Mystery of Golgotha in a form that can be received, not only by those who adhere to the older Christian tradition, but by all men on the earth.

Anthroposophy did not come to found sects or new religions. It came to call to life again what is the religion of humanity, the synthesis of all religions, the religion that is already there — Christianity. Not only is it able to call Christianity into fresh life, but for those who have been bereft of Christianity by modern science and the doubts arising from it, it is able to bring about, in the fullest sense, a resurrection of the religious life. Amongst all the other life-giving forces, Anthroposophy is able at this present time to enliven us and to bring about the resurrection of religious experience for all mankind.